MONEY PALAVER

An Immigrant's Common-Sense Approach to Money Matters

Eric G. Amankwah, ChFC

Content Editing by Kyei Amoako
Proofreading by Albert Akonu-Atta
Cover Design and Layout by Ryan Magada

Money Palaver/ Eric Amankwah
ISBN 978-0-9998312-8-1 (Paperback)

To
Shemaine,
Gabrielle,
Danielle,
Eric, and
Michelle

TABLE OF CONTENTS

Introduction

Introduction

MONEY PALAVER

Introduction

MONEY PALAVER

Introduction

MONEY PALAVER

Introduction

MONEY PALAVER

Introduction

MONEY PALAVER

Introduction

MONEY PALAVER

Introduction

MONEY PALAVER

Introduction

MONEY PALAVER

Introduction

MONEY PALAVER

Introduction

MONEY PALAVER

MONEY PALAVER

MONEY PALAVER

MONEY PALAVER

MONEY PALAVER

MONEY PALAVER

MONEY PALAVER

MONEY PALAVER

MONEY PALAVER

MONEY PALAVER

MONEY PALAVER

MONEY PALAVER

MONEY PALAVER

MONEY PALAVER

MONEY PALAVER

MONEY PALAVER

MONEY PALAVER

MONEY PALAVER

MONEY PALAVER

MONEY PALAVER

MONEY PALAVER

MONEY PALAVER

MONEY PALAVER

MONEY PALAVER

MONEY PALAVER

MONEY PALAVER

MONEY PALAVER

MONEY PALAVER

MONEY PALAVER

MONEY PALAVER

MONEY PALAVER

MONEY PALAVER

MONEY PALAVER

MONEY PALAVER

MONEY PALAVER

MONEY PALAVER

MONEY PALAVER